What Was It Before It Melted?

by Kristen McCurry

T0084487

PEBBLE
a capstone imprint

What do you think these things were
before they melted?

Take a guess,
then turn each page to find out!

What was it?

 turn to see

What was it?

turn
to see

An ice pop.

Icy treats melt fast
on a hot day!

What was it?

turn
to see

Did you guess snowman?

Snow melts when
the weather warms.

What was it?

turn
to see

Cheese.

Melted cheese can

stretch!

What was it?

turn
to see

What was it?

turn
to see

Chocolate.

Heating chocolate makes it melt.

Yum!

What was it?

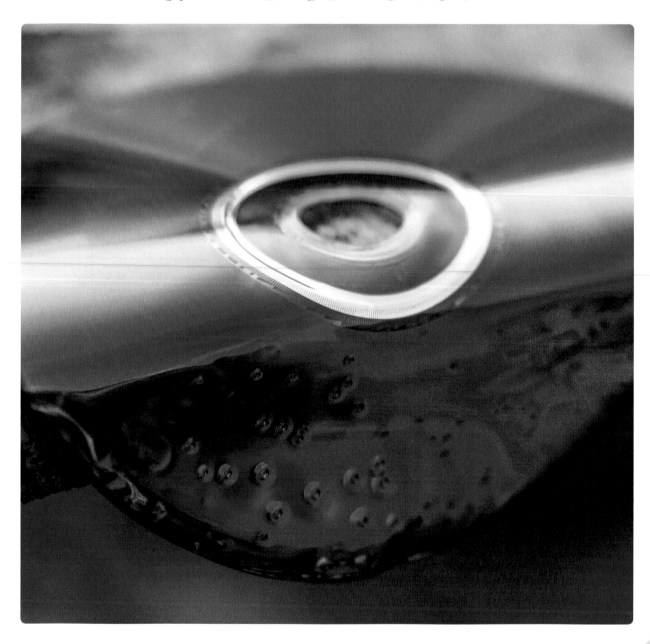

turn
to see

What was it?

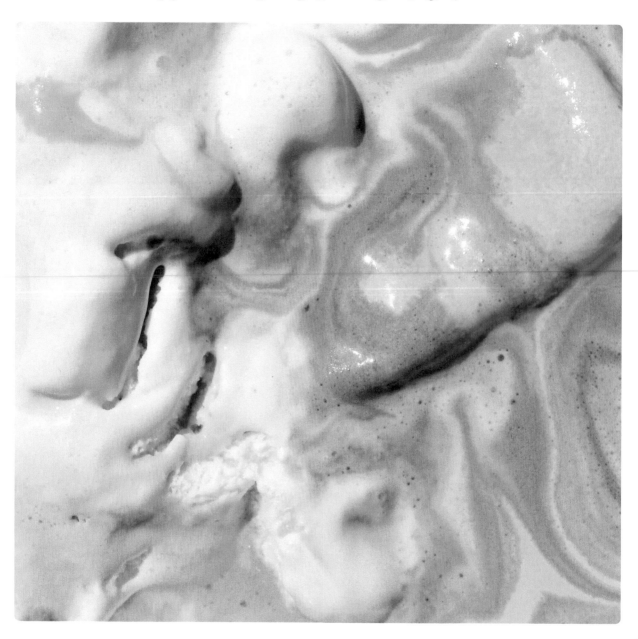

turn
to see

What was it?

turn
to see

What was it?

turn
to see

Steel.

Old steel can be melted and made into new steel parts.

What was it?

turn
to see

Marshmallows.

Roasting marshmallows makes them soft and **gooey!**

What was it?

 turn
to see

What was it?

 turn to see

Sand.

A kind of sand can be melted to make glass.

What was it?

 turn to see

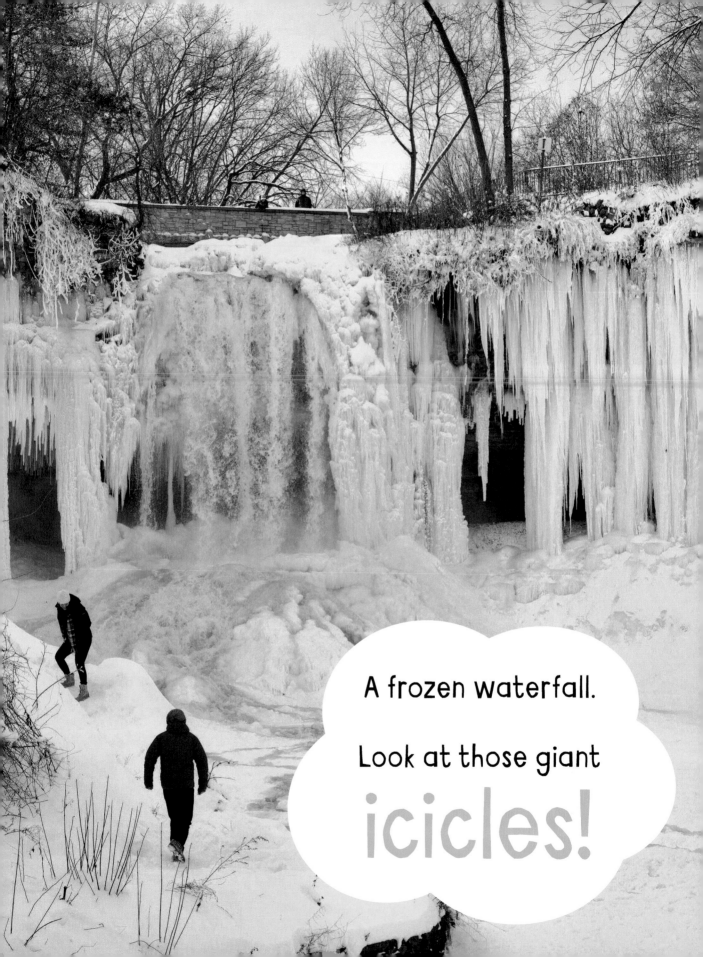

A frozen waterfall.

Look at those giant icicles!

Good job! Try all the books in this series!

What Was It Before It Was Smashed?
by Kristen McCurry

A turn-and-see book ➯

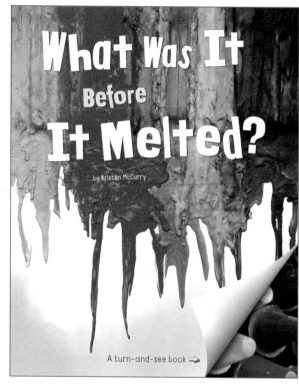

What Was It Before It Melted?
by Kristen McCurry

A turn-and-see book ➯

What Was It Before It Got Wet?
by Kristen McCurry

A turn-and-see book ➯

What Was It Before It Was Cut?
by Kristen McCurry

A turn-and-see book ➯

Pebble Sprout is published by Pebble, an imprint of Capstone.
1710 Roe Crest Drive
North Mankato, Minnesota 56003
www.capstonepub.com

Copyright © 2020 by Capstone. All rights reserved. No part of this publication may be reproduced in whole or in part, or stored in a retrieval system, or transmitted in any form or by any means, electronic, mechanical, photocopying, recording, or otherwise, without written permission of the publisher.

Library of Congress Cataloging-in-Publication Data.
Names: McCurry, Kristen, author. Title: What was it before it melted? / by Kristen McCurry. Description: North Mankato, Mannesota : Pebble, [2020] | Series: What was it? | Audience: Ages 4-8 | Audience: Grades K-1 | Summary: "Guess the melting mess! These photo puzzles challenge pre-readers to determine what items were before they melted. Gooey, oozing science mysteries!"— Provided by publisher. Identifiers: LCCN 2019044082 (print) | LCCN 2019044083 (ebook) | ISBN 9781977113320 (hardcover) | ISBN 9781977120144 (paperback) | ISBN 9781977113368 (eBook pdf) Subjects: LCSH: Fusion—Juvenile literature. | Melting points—Juvenile literature. Classification: LCC QC303 .M33 2020 (print) | LCC QC303 (ebook) | DDC 536/.42—dc23

LC record available at https://lccn.loc.gov/2019044082
LC ebook record available at https://lccn.loc.gov/2019044083

Designer: Sarah Bennett
Media Researcher: Eric Gohl
Production Specialist: Tori Abraham

Image credits
Alamy: Gina Kelly, 30, Stockimo/bradphoria, 7; iStockphoto: Christin Lola, 18, francisblack, 26, goldenKB, 6; Shutterstock: Abby Blumhardt, 23, Africa Studio, 20, Alexandr Makarov, 19, AMB-MD Photography, 29, Annette Shaff, cover, Anton Watman, 15, barmalini, 24, Benoit Daoust, 27, botulinum21, cover (bottom right), Bozena Fulawka, 28, Chaikom, 1, Christin Lola, 17, David Herraez Calzada, 16, Freer, 5, gorillaimages, 8, JGA, 11, kaband, 13, Lutsenko_Oleksandr, 12, mikeledray, 25, Pair Srinrat, 9, pathdoc, Shi Yali, 22, ULKASTUDIO, 10, Vitaliy Krasovskiy, 4, Yongyut Rukkachatsuwa, 21, Yuliya L, 3

Design Elements: Shutterstock